Maiyang Saridjo

What Do You Say?

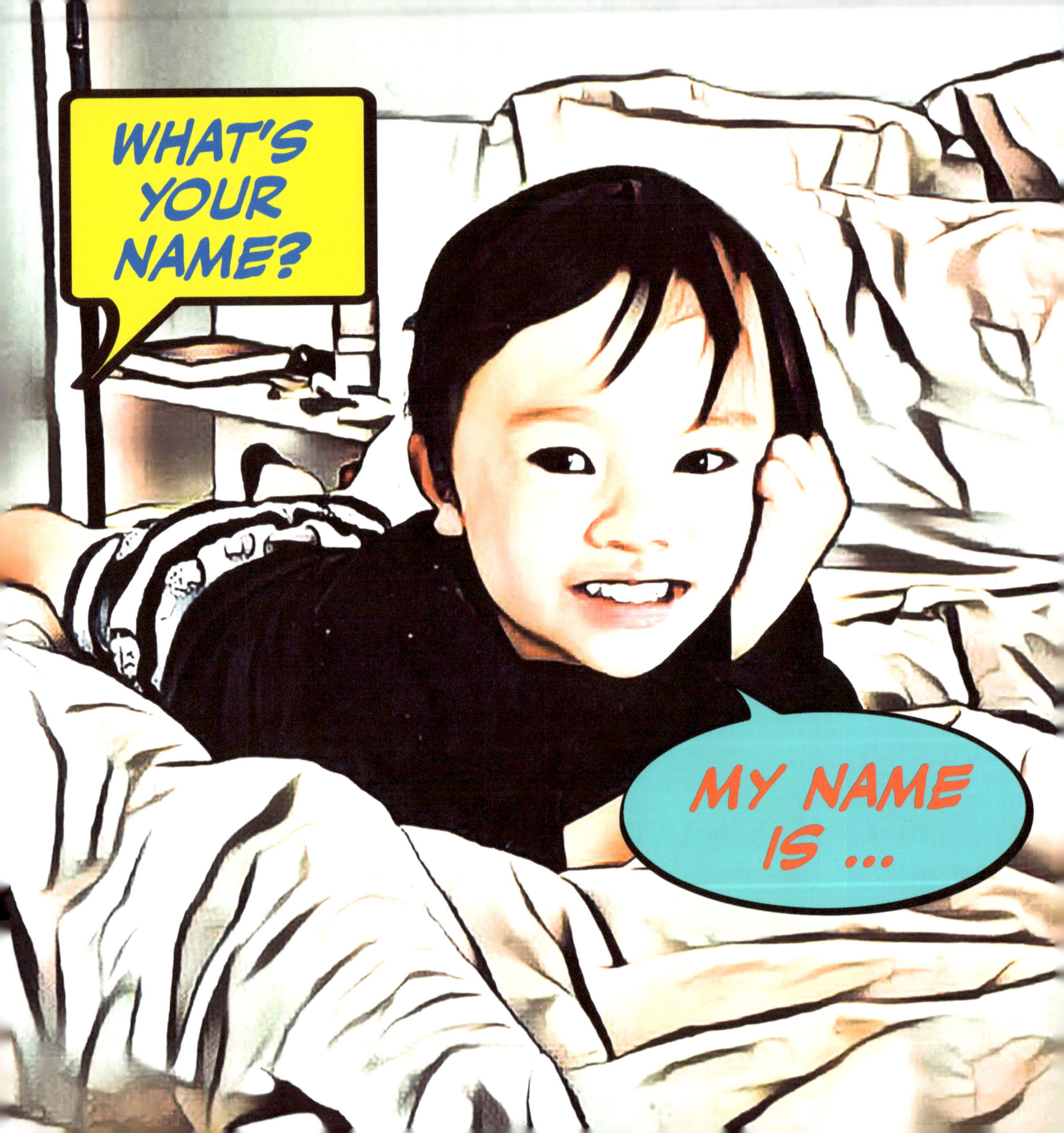
WHAT'S YOUR NAME?
MY NAME IS ...

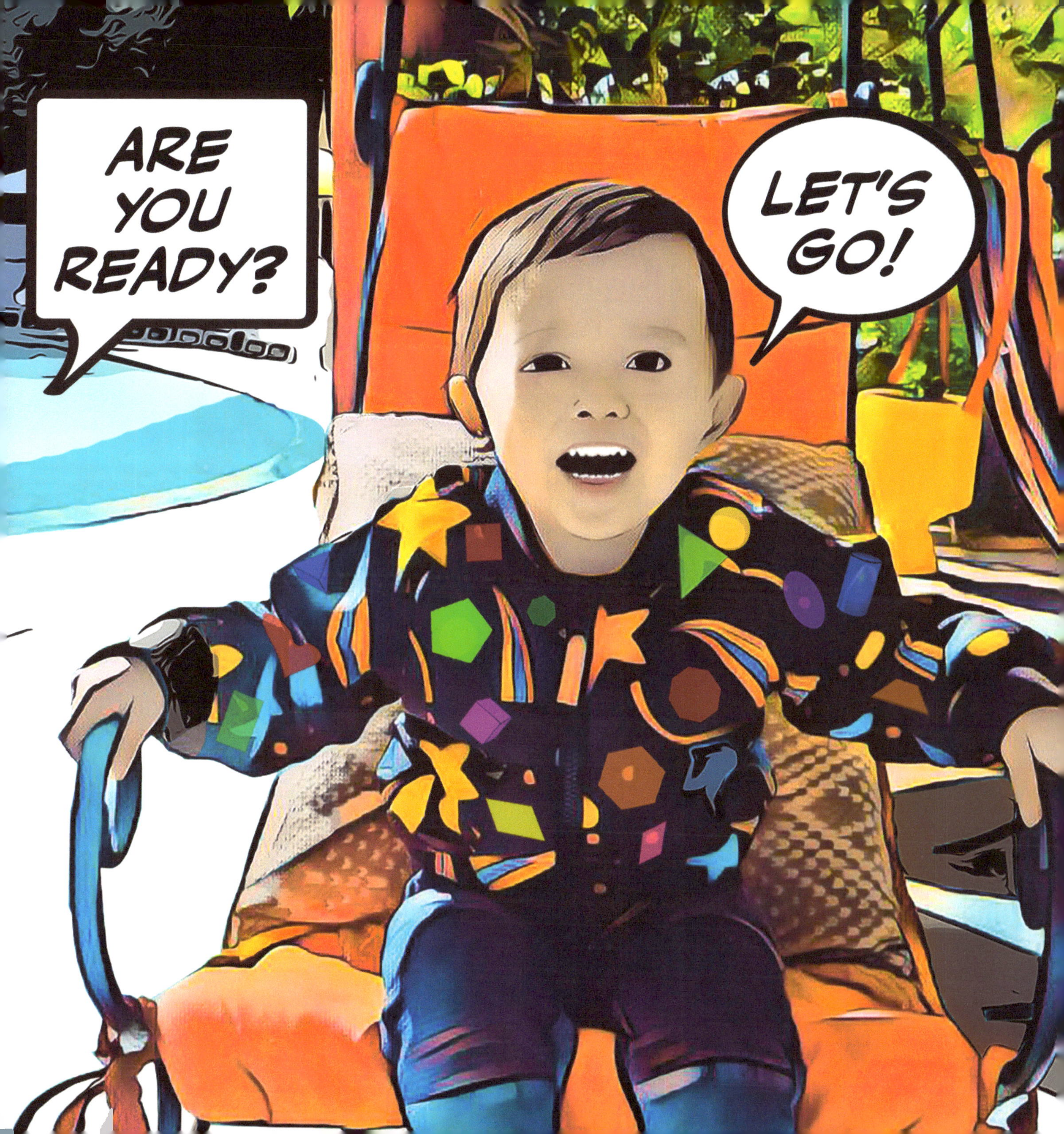
ARE YOU READY?
LET'S GO!

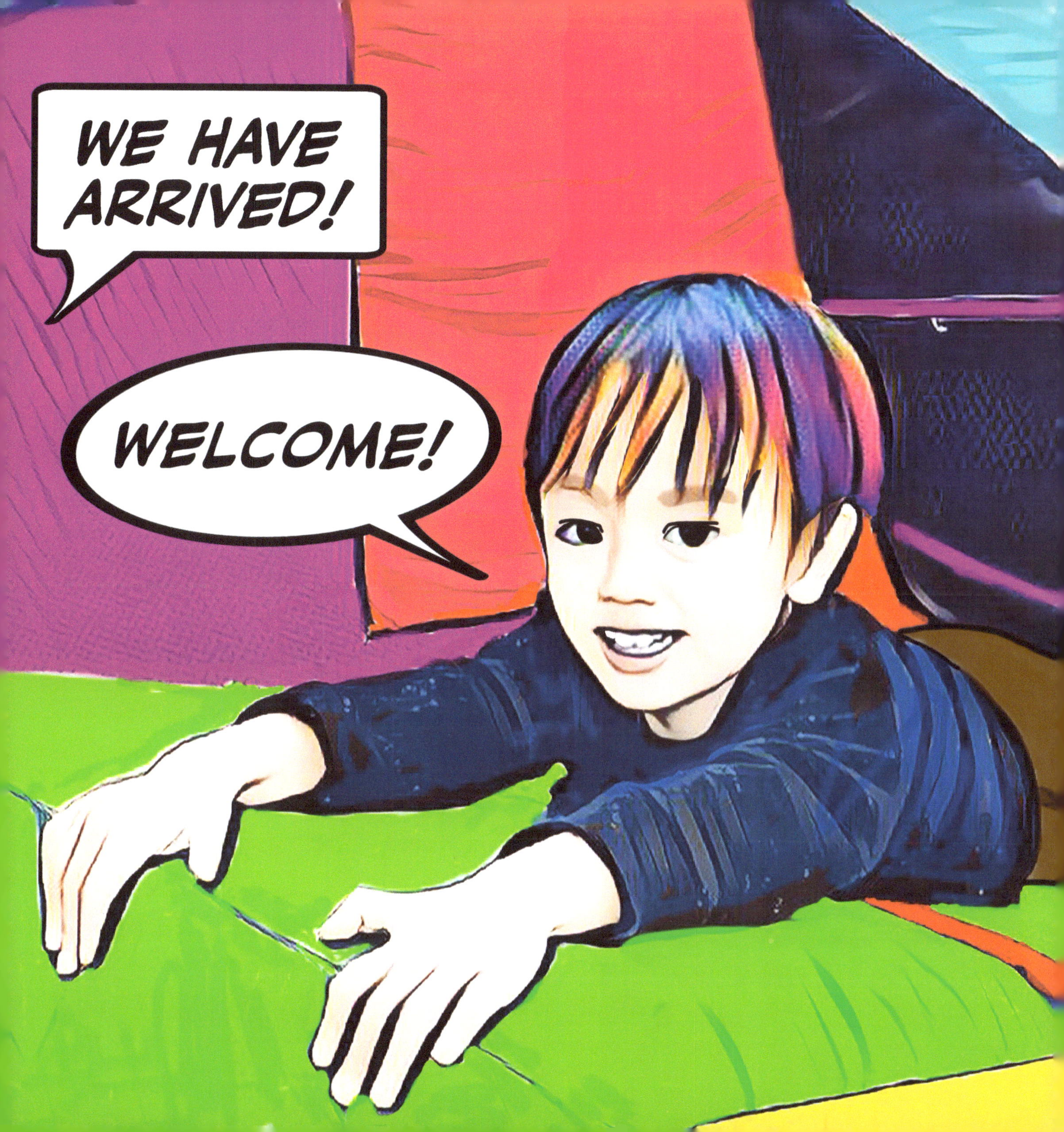
WE HAVE ARRIVED!
WELCOME!

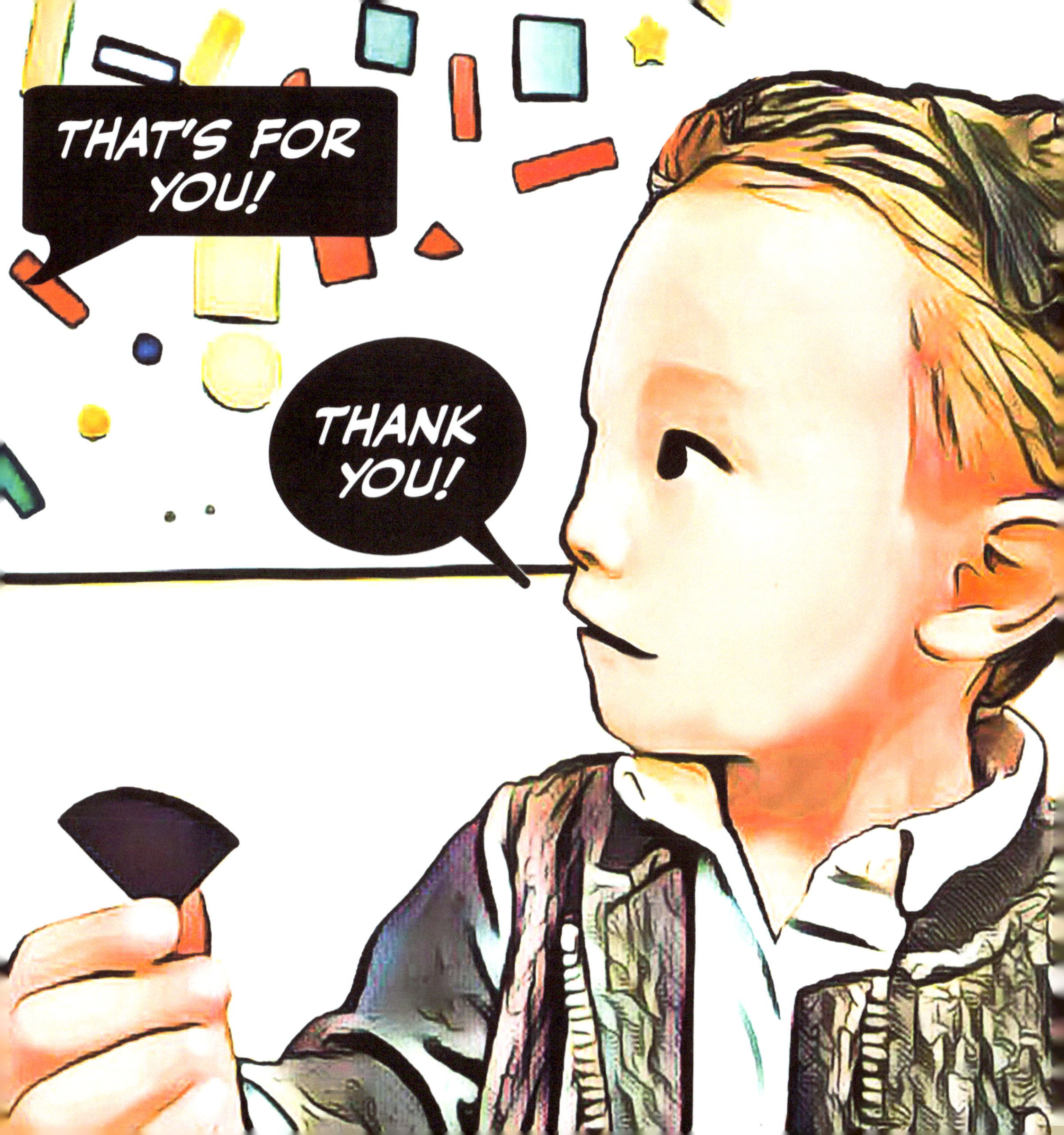
THAT'S FOR YOU!
THANK YOU!

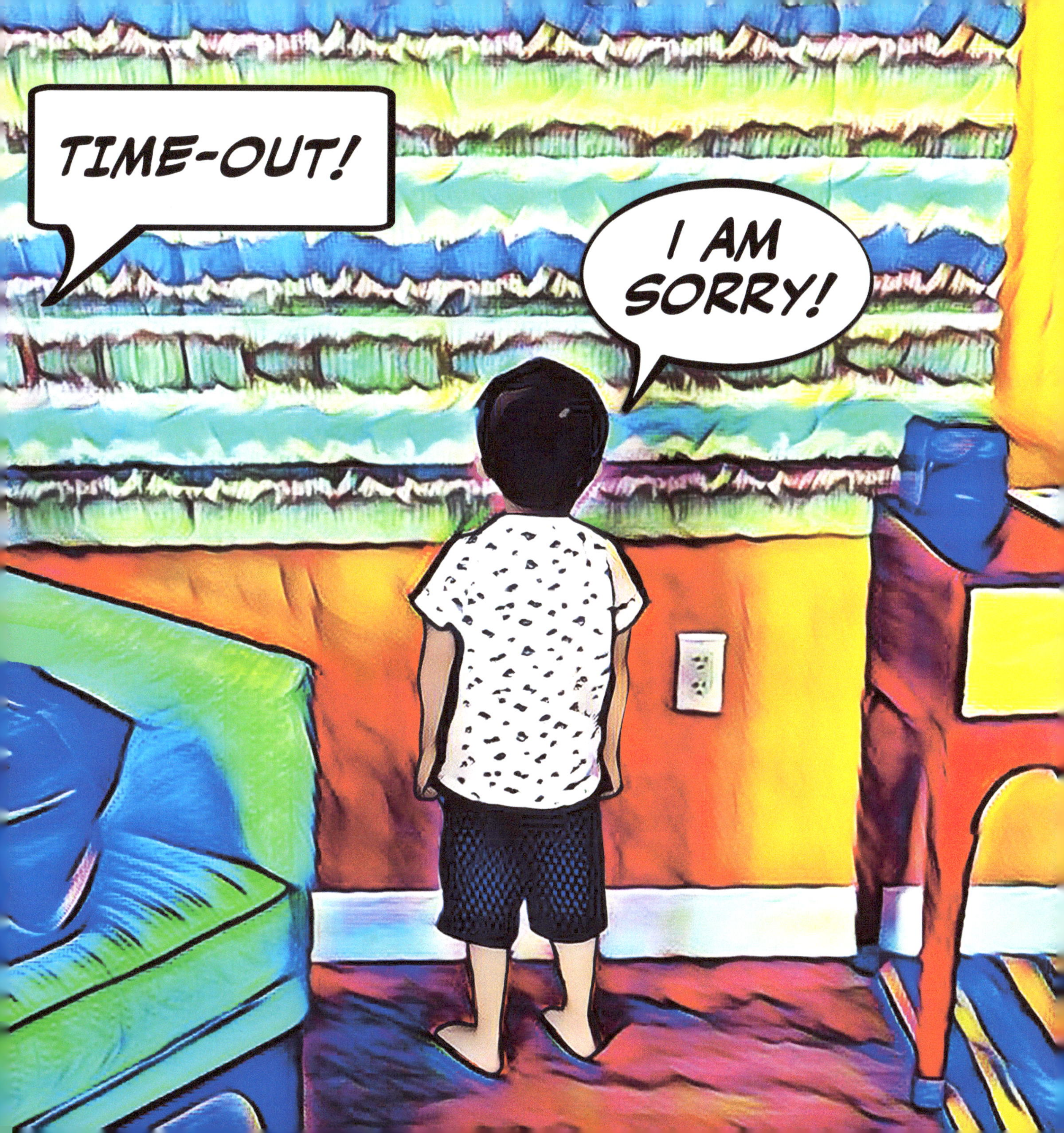
TIME-OUT!
I AM SORRY!

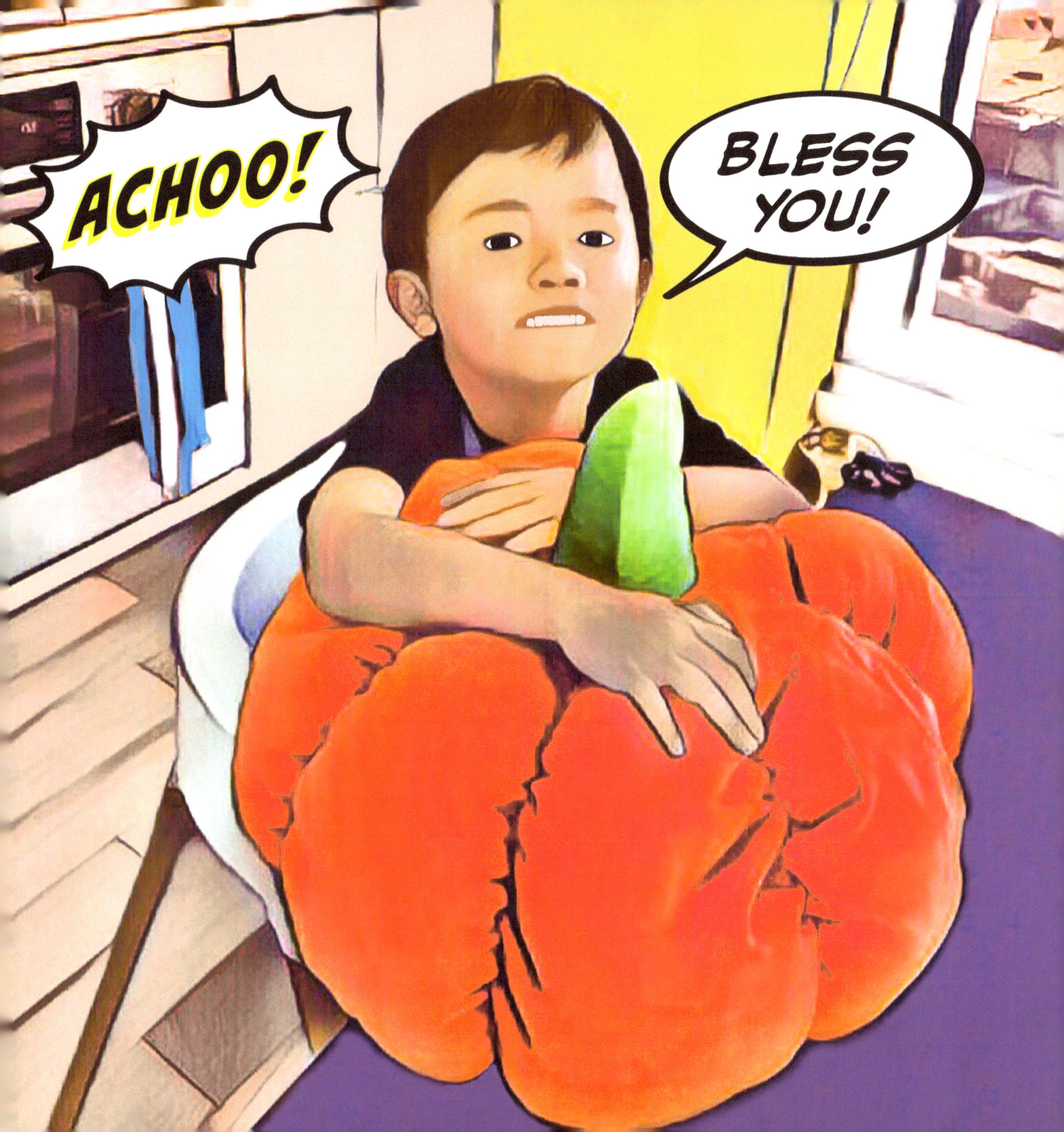
ACHOO!
BLESS YOU!

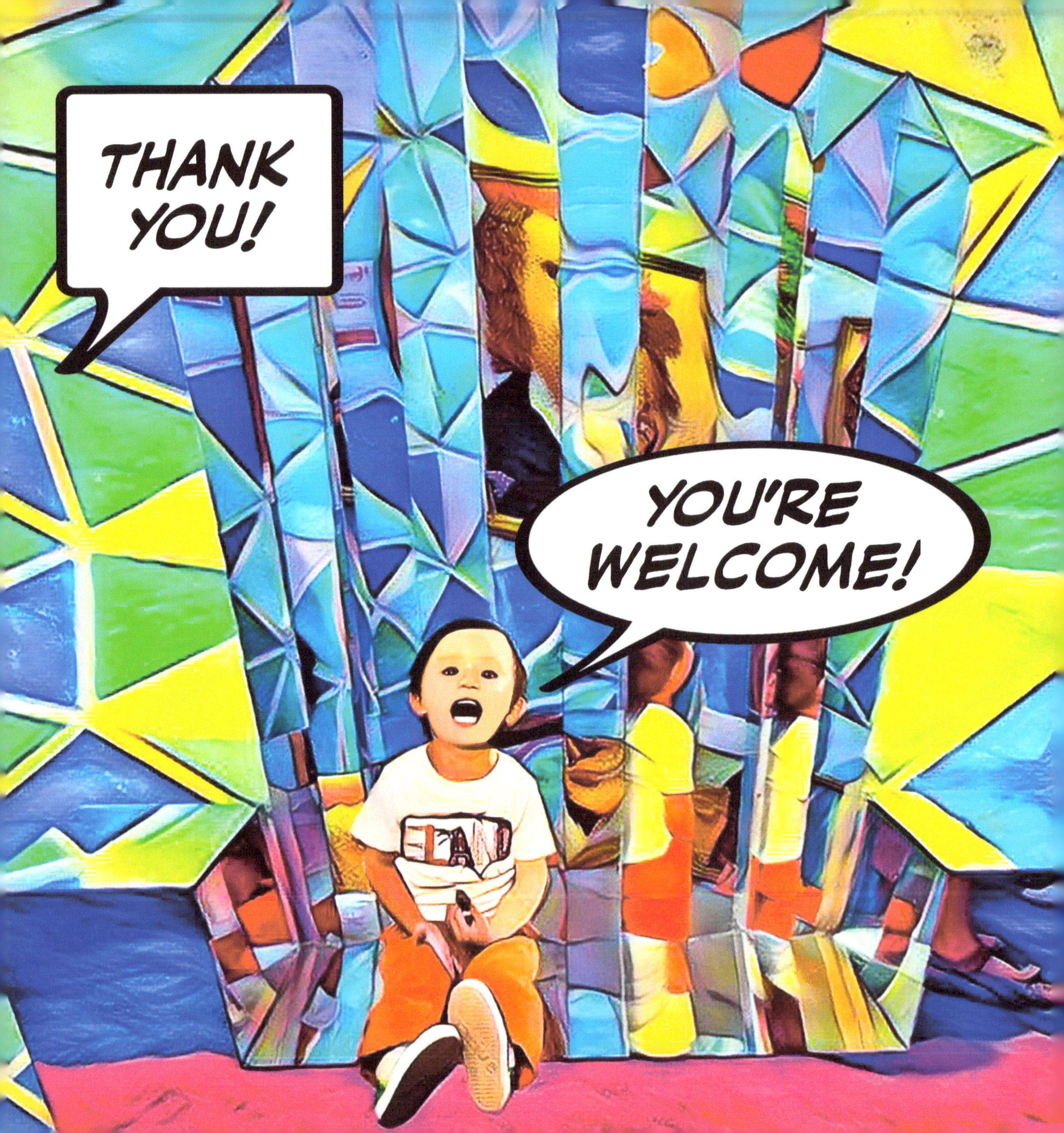
THANK YOU!
YOU'RE WELCOME!

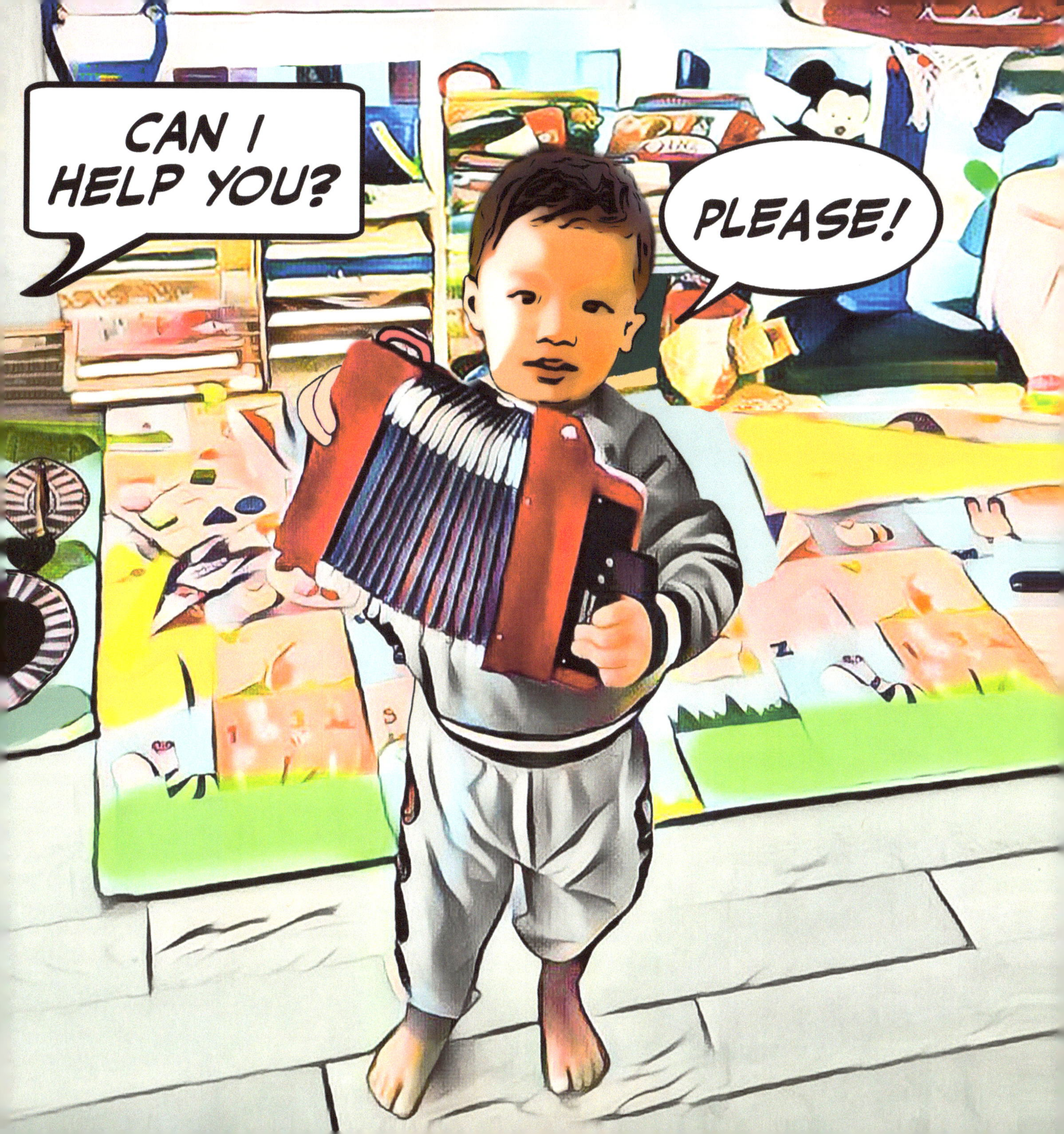
CAN I HELP YOU?
PLEASE!

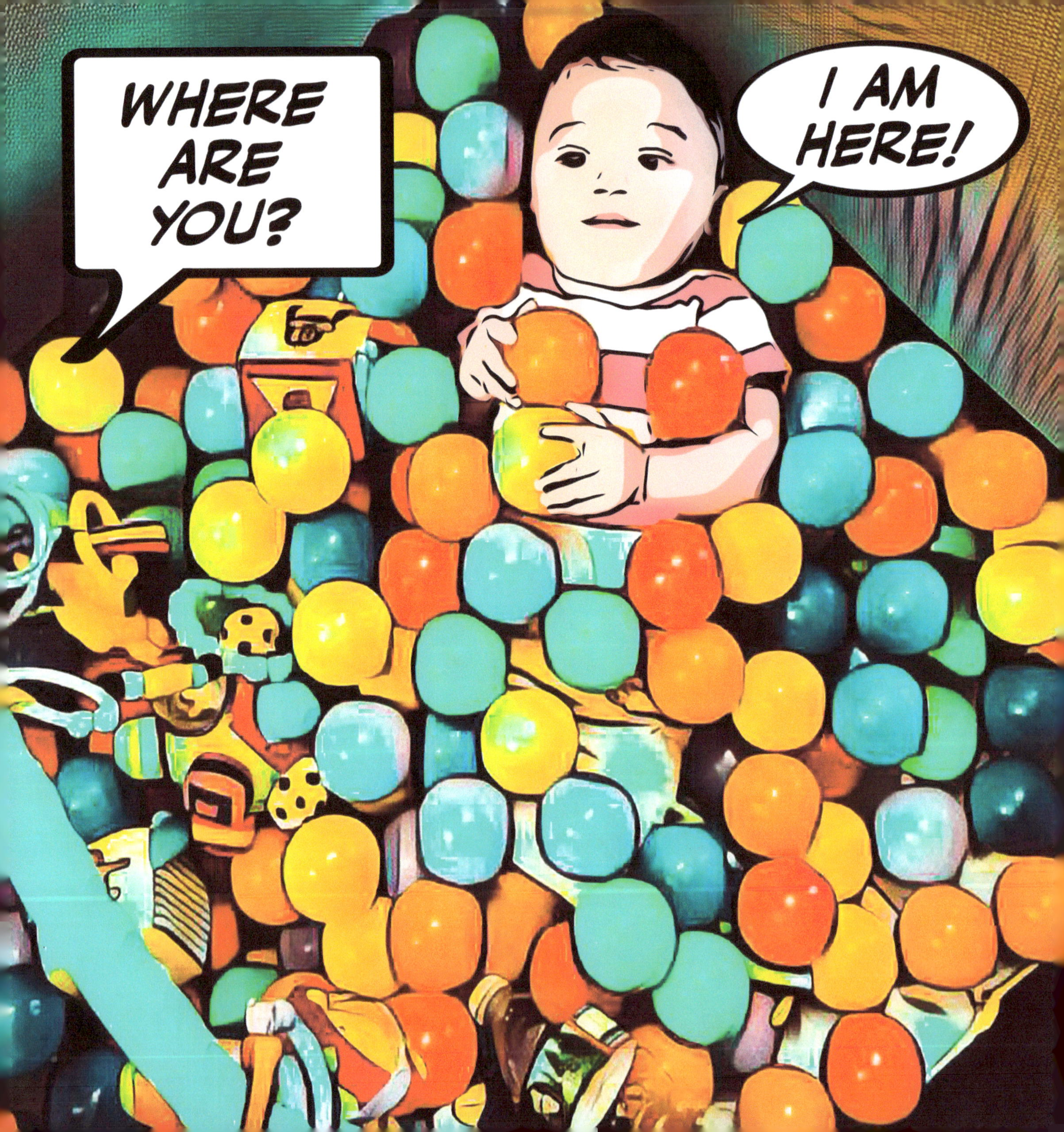
WHERE ARE YOU?
I AM HERE!

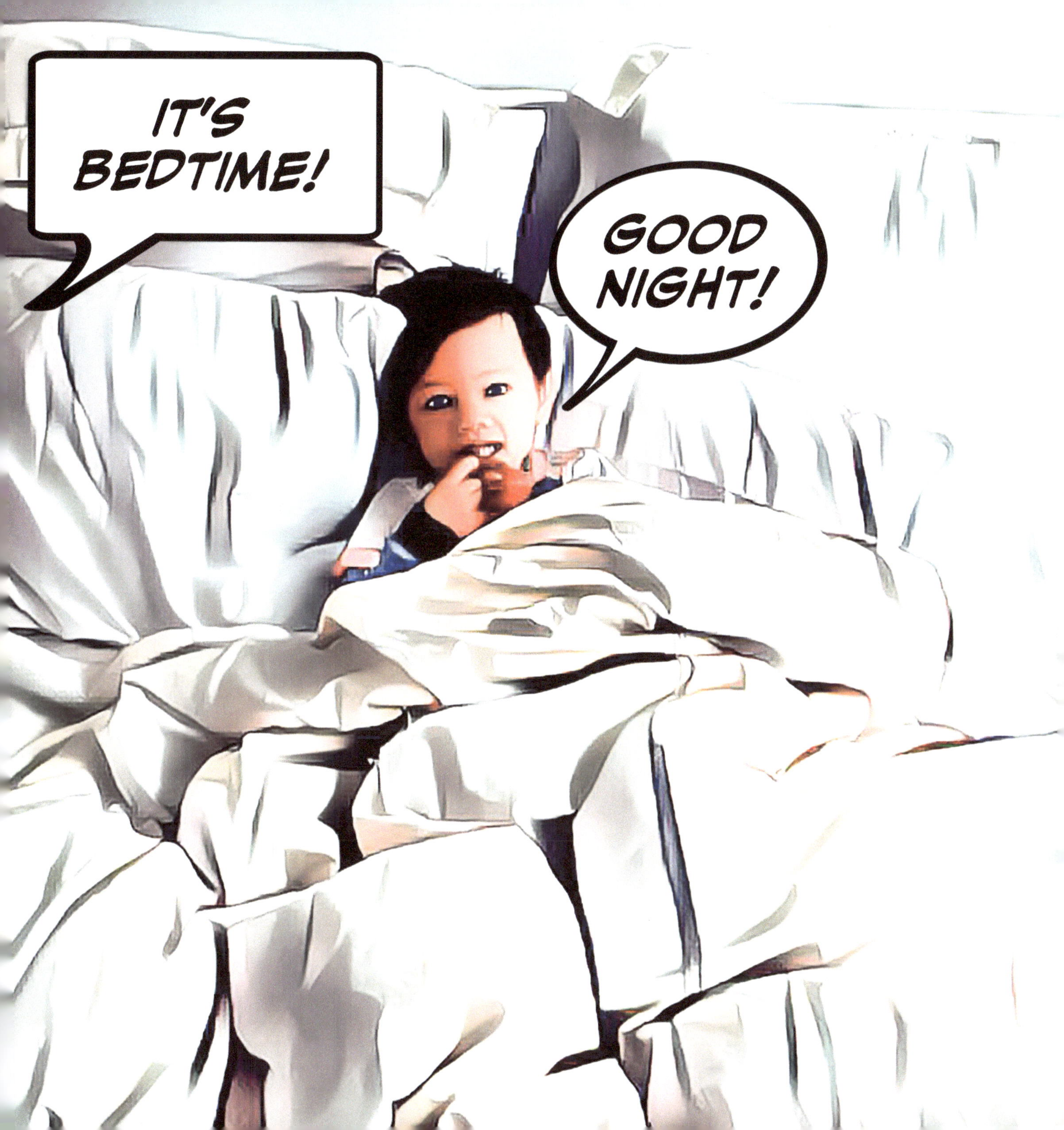
IT'S BEDTIME!
GOOD NIGHT!

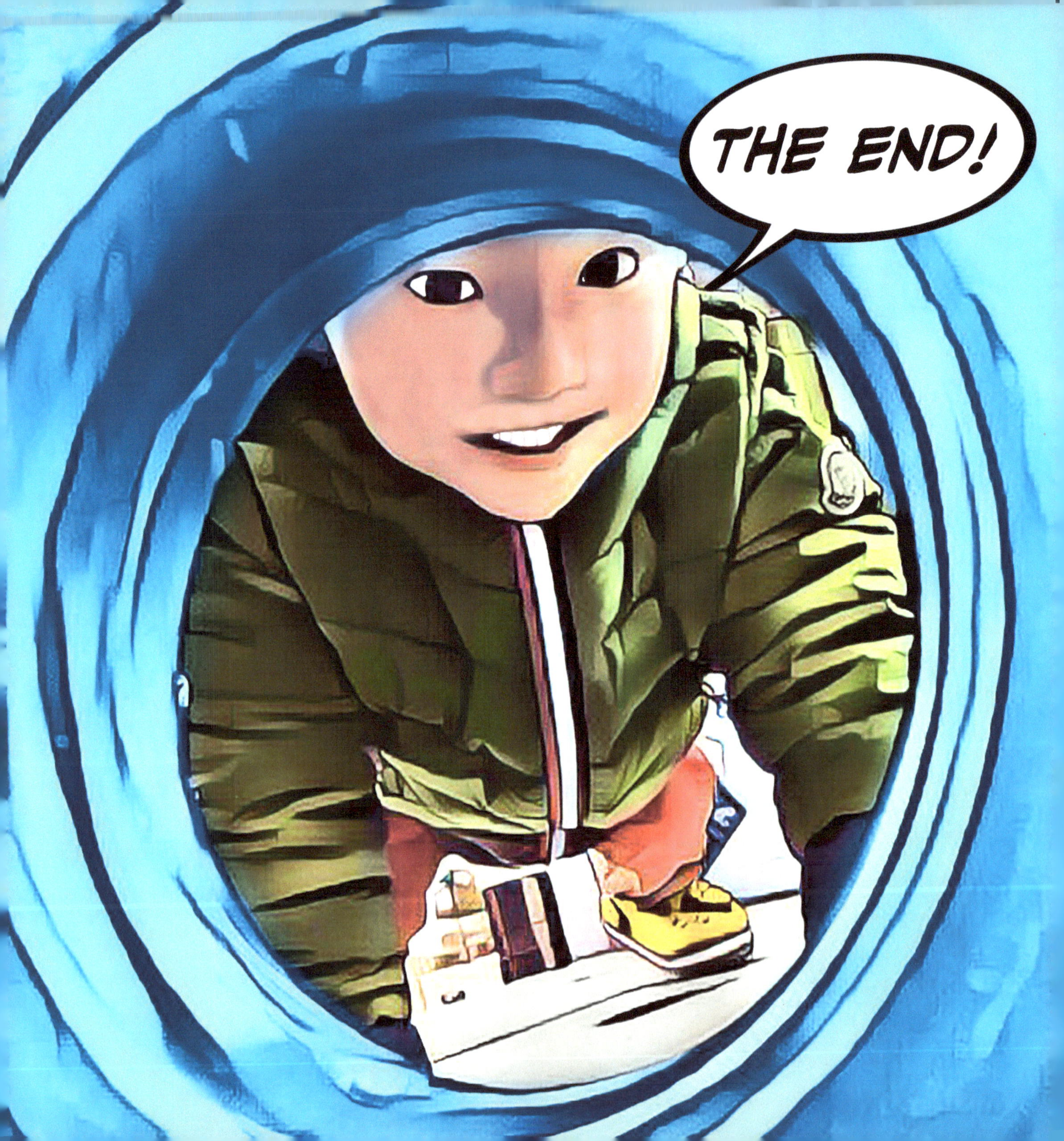
THE END!

What Do You Say, ...
when someone says:

THANK YOU!

Adult

YOU'RE WELCOME!

Child

Teach your little ones simple basic responses through this engaging Q&A book that gives toddlers a head start on manners. The common straight-forward questions will engage them to answer in a nice way and boost their social skills.

The reader starts by describing the words/actions on the left of the page (e.g. "What do you say when you answer the phone?"),and the child's response is the words on the right of the page (e.g. "Hello, who's speaking?").

Children will immediately respond to the colorful illustrations and be sure to look for letters, planets, shapes and other learning opportunities throughout the book!

22 pages of illustrations to create your own stories with your tots!
The large fonts are perfect for early readers!

Maiyang Saridjo [my-ahng • sa-reed-jo]

Also known as Maiya, she is the author and illustrator of Rainbow in My Room and the brain behind the Saridjo™ brand. She lives with her family and two cats in TriBeCa, New York, among a pile of her innovative products and creations.

THE READER

THE CHILD

FOR ADAM GIBRAN, WHO LOVES HIS ALPHABETS, SHAPES, NUMBERS AND PLANETS.

DEDICATED TO MY FATHER, MR. H. ATAK SARIDJO.

Text and illustrations © 2019 by Saridjo Imports LLC

Maiyang Saridjo reserves the right to be identified as the author and the illustrator of this work.

ISBN 978-0578442679 • Library of Congress Control Number: 2019901075

This edition first printing, January 2019.

www.ingramcontent.com/pod-product-compliance
Lightning Source LLC
Chambersburg PA
CBHW041242040426
42445CB00004B/123